Know Your Enemy
How To Combat and Overcome
Demonic Forces

Know Your Enemy
How To Combat and Overcome Demonic Forces

by

Norvel Hayes

Harrison House
Tulsa, Oklahoma

Know Your Enemy —
How To Combat and Overcome Demonic Forces
ISBN 0-89274-757-9
Copyright © 1990 by Norvel Hayes
P. O. Box 1379
Cleveland, Tennessee 37311

Published by Harrison House, Inc.
P. O. Box 35035
Tulsa, Oklahoma 74153

Contents

And he said unto them, Go ye into all the world, and preach the gospel to every creature.

He that believeth and is baptized shall be saved; but he that believeth not shall be damned.

And these signs shall follow them that believe; In my name shall they cast out devils; they shall speak with new tongues;

They shall take up serpents; and if they drink any deadly thing, it shall not hurt them; they shall lay hands on the sick, and they shall recover.

Mark 16:15-18

Know Your Enemy
How To Combat and Overcome Demonic Forces

1

The Second Most Important Subject

The most important subject in the world is Jesus, and after that, the next most important is your enemy. You need to know where the devil comes from, where demons come from, how they operate, and who they attack.

You need to know that demons operate through generations of the same family. Some people reading this book have demonic problems that have "run" (or shown up in person after person) in their families for generations.

Demons are personalities without bodies.

A demon is desperate for a body, and the number one target is a human body. They will operate through animals to a certain degree, but they prefer to use the bodies of men and women. Mankind is God's number-one prize creation, and demons hate God.

Satan and thousands times thousands of demons are moving through the air. Many thousands of them do not have bodies in which to live. A third of the angels in heaven were thrown out when Satan fell. (Rev. 12:4,7-9.) We do not know how many that was, but we do know it was a multitude.

In this chapter, I want to deal with the particular kind of demon — or the particular assignment of many demons — which is the primary way Satan deceives the Church. I have taught in many churches around the country — and this may surprise many people — but there is more room for demons in full-gospel churches than in denominational churches!

Most churches do not know very much about the devil at all. All they know is that he is mean. Satan has so many ministers and so many Christians deceived! He is the number one deceiver on earth. He does not want you to see him as the devil. He wants you to think that whatever happens to you or whatever way you are is God's fault or your own fault. He does not want to be recognized.

He wants to stay in the background and have you not talk about him or know that he is anywhere around.

Have you ever heard someone get behind the pulpit and say, "I just want to talk about Jesus all the time. I don't want to talk about the devil."

That is exactly what the devil wants to hear you say. He does not ever want you to know he is operating in you or in your church. If you do not expose him from the Word of God and do not know what God says about him, you will never know your enemy.

How would you parents like it if the United States Army drafted your son at eighteen years of age, then immediately took him overseas and dropped him by parachute into some war zone? If the army did not put him through basic training, he would not know how to protect himself, how to fire a gun, or even how to dig a foxhole. He would not know how to do anything. If he were fortunate, he might live about three minutes.

Exactly the same thing will happen to you in different phases of your life if you do not know your enemy. You must know how to deal with him.

Some people do not recognize their enemy in sickness and disease. They think those things are "God's will," or that God allowed those things to afflict them — or even put sickness and disease on them — "to teach me a lesson."

God does *not* do it. The Bible teaches that all *good* things that ever come to you come down from heaven from the Father of Life. All good things come from God, and all things that come to destroy you, to cause you harm or confusion, or to bring heartaches and trouble into your life come from the devil and his workers.

Demons and foul spirits will oppress you if you allow it. They will possess you if they can. However, a devil can never possess you unless you participate with him or yield to his temptations. Begin participating in some sin, and he will have a foothold in you.

Satan deceives churches, and *the* Church, with religion: doing their own thing in their own time and by their own will, through their own way. God wants us to do *His* thing in *His* time and in *His* way.

Deceived Churches and Christians

"I, I, me, me."

"This is the way we do it."

"This is the way I do it."

Who cares how *you* do it? Let God set up that church the way He wants to set it up. He wants you, a born-again believer, to respond to Him the way He says. He wants you to put first things first.

You will never build a church for God that will be successful until you come to the place where you will spend adequate time praying in front of Almighty God.

Also, you must learn how to worship and praise the Lord, then teach your congregation this.

If you will do this, I will guarantee that the Spirit of God will begin to draw people into your work. No man can come to Jesus, the Bible says, unless the Father draws him. (John 6:44.) If you pray, praise God, and worship Him, I promise you that the Spirit of God will draw people to that church.

He also deceives churches with doctrines, inter- pretations of God's Word that range from having a little error to being almost entirely in error. Entire movements and denominations down through the last two thousand years have been deceived by doctrines.

If the doctrine of your church is that God does not heal today, then a sick person asking for prayer is laughed at and told, "We don't do that here!" The sick wanting to be prayed for are treated as if they are in error and into something weird, when really those who do not believe in laying hands on the sick are into something weird, something unscriptural.

A friend of mine went to a denominational church in my hometown after hearing me and Kenneth E. Hagin preach a few times. He knew the church did not have any anointing oil, so he bought some and took it over.

He said, "Pastor, here is some oil. According to James 5:14 and 15, if you will anoint me with oil and pray for me, I will be healed."

The pastor said, "Ah, Mr. Green, you know we are not supposed to do that now. That was for back in Bible days. If we were supposed to do that now, there would be no need for doctors, hospitals, and nurses."

That is the reason so many Christians die before their time. God will let you do your own thing, if you want to. He does not like it, but He will let you. Paul wrote to Timothy about these times:

> **Now the Spirit speaketh expressly, that in the latter times some shall depart from the faith, giving heed to seducing spirits, and doctrines of devils.**
>
> **1 Timothy 4:1**

When those seducing spirits get into your mind they will make you think all sorts of things. You will dream up all types of church services and think God is pleased with them. You will hardly do anything the Bible says, but come up with all sorts of programs and activities of men. You have gotten completely away from the doctrine of Christ and gone with the doctrines of men.

The one thing the Head of the Church does not want you to get involved in is doctrines of men. That church where I attended as a child might have had the aisles full of people wanting to give their lives to Jesus. However, if they were sick, it was too bad. "We don't do that anymore!" was the answer they got.

"Cast out devils? Are you kidding? We would not get involved in that stuff. That's weird!"

We called our Sunday morning service the "11 o'clock worship hour," but we never worshiped anything.

Obey the Doctrine of God*

What is the doctrine of God? Matthew 15:8 states:

This people draweth nigh unto me with their mouth, and honoureth me with their lips; but their heart is far from me.

The doctrine of God states: Put Him first. If you will put first things first, you can walk in the peace of God.

If you want to know God better, find some friends who know Him better than you do and hang around them. Watch the company you keep. You may have some friends you need to move away from.

The devil works heavily with doctrines of men throughout the human race. It seems as if the "colder" the church, the more people they have! I used to love to attend a cold church. I was not required to do anything. Forget doctrines of men and come to God as yourself, as an individual.

The Spirit and the Word agree.

---

*See Titus 2:10, 2 John 9,8, Hebrews 6:1,2.

2

Where Did Satan Come From?

First of all, you need to know where the devil came from. God created everything; therefore, He created Satan. Originally, the devil was a very beautiful being. As far as I can find out, he probably was created before anything else. Certainly, he was created before the earth and man. We do not have as much information as we might like to have on the devil, but God gave us all that we need to know.

There are a lot of things about heaven and hell that we would like to know a little more about. We would like for God to come down to earth and write us a third-grade-level book and just spell out everything for us.

Well, God *has* written us a book called the Bible, and it has in it everything we really need to know — not everything we might like to know. Therefore, everything we *need* to know about the devil is in the Bible.

If God created the devil, and God can never create anything that is not good and perfect, what caused him to fall? He fell on account of his beauty. He developed pride, and that led to self-will, to lustful desires and greed for power. Then he moved into rebellion against his Creator. And that process is the same one human beings take.

Look at Ezekiel 28:13

> **Thou hast been in Eden the garden of God; every precious stone was thy covering, the sardius, topaz, and the diamond, the beryl, the onyx, and the jasper, the sapphire, the emerald, and the carbuncle, and gold: the workmanship of thy tabrets and of thy pipes was prepared in thee in the day that thou wast created.**

Thou art the anointed cherub that covereth; and I have set thee so: thou wast upon the holy mountain of God; thou hast walked up and down in the midst of the stones of fire.

Thou wast perfect in thy ways from the day that thou wast created, till iniquity was found in thee.

By the multitude of thy merchandise they have filled the midst of thee with violence, and thou hast sinned: therefore I will cast thee as profane out of the mountain of God: and I will destroy thee, O covering cherub, from the midst of the stones of fire.

Thine heart was lifted up because of thy beauty, thou hast corrupted thy wisdom by reason of thy brightness: I will cast thee to the ground, I will lay thee before kings, that they may behold thee.

Thou hast defiled thy sanctuaries by the multitude of thine iniquities, by the iniquity of thy traffick; therefore will I bring forth a fire from the midst of thee, it shall devour thee, and I will bring thee to ashes upon the earth in the sight of all them that behold thee.

All they that know thee among the people shall be astonished at thee: thou shalt be a terror, and never shalt thou be any more.

Ezekiel 28:13-19

The supernatural being, who is our adversary and whom we call *Satan* or the devil, was created with a talent for music. That is the reason some Bible scholars believe that, at one time, Satan was an angel of light, who sang praise and led the other angels in singing praises to God Almighty.

Even today, you will notice that demons have the same kind of musical talent. Satan still has that talent, although he has fallen from heaven. Running back and forth through the atmosphere, their music and type of dancing permeates various kinds of modern music: rock, heavy metal, punk, and so forth.

Pride Goes Before a Fall

Iniquity was found in the "anointed cherub," and by iniquity is meant greed, lust, possessiveness, pride, selfish-

18

ness, and all the other carnal and soulish sins. By the multitude, or the quantity, of these things — "thy merchandise" — Satan was filled with violence. Those iniquities, which have been found in mankind since Adam and Eve chose Satan's way instead of God's way, abounded in the being of light until he started a revolution, a rebellion.

The devil and his demons try to get every human being to become like them. The Lord has told me to warn Christians that the devil works in us and around us to cause pride to rise up, so that all of the multitude of iniquities might be developed within us.

If you find yourself thinking of your beauty, or your goodness, or your talent, or your spirituality in terms of pride, stop yourself! Then, because the words of our mouths are so powerful, just begin to confess that you are not anything without Jesus.

Begin to say, "Without Jesus, I am nothing. Without You, Jesus, I'm nothing. I'm totally helpless. Whatever I am that is good, You are the cause of it, Jesus. Whatever I do that is truly good will be of Your doing."

Even those evangelists or preachers who operate under a heavy anointing from the Holy Spirit can be subtly brought to take the credit for that. If they succumb to that kind of spiritual pride, to mixing flesh with the glory of God, their ministry will be destroyed.

I could tell you of good men, evangelists, all over this country who used to operate in the power of God. They used to have a ministry, a mission, but you never hear of them anymore. Perhaps they do preach once in a while, but their public ministry essentially has disappeared.

The reason is that they allowed some demon to plant thoughts in them of their own abilities, their own goodness, and pride rose up.

Do not let yourself think that you are something *in yourself*, because if you do, you will fall. On the other hand, you are not an unworthy worm. You are a vessel which carries the greatest Treasure in the world: Jesus Christ; therefore, you are valuable, *but only because of the Treasure and His transforming power.*

The Deceiver

Now let's look at Revelation 12:

> And there was war in heaven: Michael and his angels fought against the dragon; and the dragon fought and his angels,
>
> And prevailed not; neither was their place found any more in heaven.
>
> And the great dragon was cast out, that old serpent, called the Devil, and Satan, which deceiveth the whole world: he was cast out into the earth, and his angels were cast out with him.
>
> Revelation 12:7-9

Satan thought he was so big that he could take over heaven. He thought the angels would obey him, and some of them did. The other angels, the ones who remained faithful to God, fought the devil and his angels. And the devil and his angels were cast down into the earth.

The *earth* is where we live. And it is full of demons taking orders from Satan to steal, kill, and destroy the human race, to deceive them in every way possible.

The devil has deceived nearly the entire Church world. That is the reason it scares other Christians if you say that demons are cast out of people in your church. That sounds like a foreign language to them. Yet it is supposed to be an everyday thing.

Jesus did not put up with devils. He just cast them out and went on. If you do not believe that, read Matthew, Mark, Luke, and John, the four Gospels, and notice the number of different times Jesus cast demons out of people. Demons *had* to obey Him.

Some people have asked me, "Why don't demons obey me as quickly as they did Jesus?"

They do not obey you, because you do not operate in as much power as He did. Yes, you have the Holy Spirit inside you, but you do not live your life the way Jesus did. You do not have enough experience with different demons to find out the truth.

Jesus lived His life so clean, so committed to the Father, so full of faith, that He left no room for doubt. He spent a lot of time in prayer, sometimes all night long. When is the last time most of us prayed all night? That is the reason demons moved when Jesus spoke. The power of the Holy Spirit had no obstacles in Him to flow around, no blockages of flesh and soul to hinder His power from coming forth.

Jesus told His disciples once that unbelief kept them from casting out a demon. (Matt. 17:20.) Also, He said that kind comes out only by prayer and fasting. (v. 21.) He knew they had not been praying very much.

The more time you spend in prayer, the more power you have inside your life. Before you ever go to the street and witness for God, if you are on a witnessing team, pray and pray and pray. Walk the floor, close your eyes, and pray in the Spirit before you ever go out and face the devil on the street.

If you would pray even thirty minutes pretty hard and strong, there is no devil in the street that can defeat you. You will be as if you have a one-track mind. More than ninety percent of all Christians have never won a soul to God, and until they begin to pray, they will not be winning one.

The hunger God placed inside you was not placed there for your own benefit, but to win souls for the Kingdom. You can turn that hunger into feeding your own spirit and become satisfied with doing your own thing spiritually. You will have no desire to win souls. You are too busy feeding yourself.

No man or woman had better go out to build churches without spending time in prayer to fight the devil.

Some mornings I wake up and the peace of God just saturates me, flowing up and down in my body. I just lie in bed and think how wonderful it is to know the Lord. The sweet Spirit of Almighty God soaks through my body and every fiber and cell is at rest.

I remember the days when I was a nervous wreck. But when God comes to visit you and lays His hand on you, you are never the same.

In a meeting once, I prayed for a woman with back problems, and God gave her a new back. That woman and her husband insisted I come and stay in their home instead of at the hotel, so I did.

While I was there, I received a vision that showed me God wanted me before I came out of my mother's womb. My mother was an old-fashioned Southern Baptist, and those people pray. I can tell you, they pray! My mother would pray and shout out in the fields around our house.

The church in which I was raised had deacons who would go down to the woods behind the church and pray for an hour before church started. They prayed as loud as they could pray. Sometimes the power of God would hit them, and they would run through the woods like wild men. They would jump gullies and just take off running.

If deacons today would do the same, they would find God's power falling and find themselves running through the woods. God has not changed. We have changed.

God will visit anyone who prays long enough. If you are sincere enough, God will visit you.

3

How I Learned To Cast Out Demons

We have established the fact that the devil was created beautiful, intelligent, and perfect by God. But, because of pride, greed, and lust, he got thrown out of heaven, taking about one-third of the angels with him.

In the air around the earth are thousands upon thousands of fallen angels without bodies — and they want yours. They will do anything to get yours. If they cannot get a human body, they will operate through animals. But their prize dwelling place is inside a human being because humans are made in the image of God. Demons so hate God they will do anything they can to hurt Him.

One of the easiest things for a human being to do is go to hell. Many, perhaps most, will go there because they will not listen to God. You have the right to go your own way, even if that way leads to hell.

It is not easy for God to get people to cast out demons, because most churches have not been teaching people how to do this, or even that it is possible in our day, until recent years. The denomination in which I grew up has thousands of churches with more than sixteen million members today. Those people know God and love God, but few of them cast out demons.

I went to church on Sunday mornings, but my attention was more on material than spiritual things. I used to think that if you had money, you would be happy. So I used to ask God to make me rich. I started out working for a sharecropper for twenty-five cents a day. In about two and a half years, I was making $100 a day.

Then I began to make $1,000 a week, then $6,000 a week. When you make that much, it does not take you very long to get what you think you want. However, when I got to where I thought I wanted to be, I was more unhappy than when I was a penniless teenager.

Money is not where happiness is. There is only one true peace, and that is when you make Jesus Lord of your life. Happiness is becoming a bondslave to Jesus, so that everything you are and have and ever will be belongs to Him. That is when you find out what life is all about.

You will always be wondering about life until you get into the Bible and learn about Jesus. The devil also is not dead, and he will try to keep you in religion and keep you from an intimate relationship with Jesus.

When I finally gave my life to God, I said, "God, You go ahead, mold me, and use me. My life is yours. I am tired of trying to find happiness in money and clubs and social life." I got on my knees while on a trip to Georgia Tech and gave my life to God completely. I wanted to know the truth.

One Truth Leads to Another

The first and best truth about God is that if we accept Jesus, we will go to heaven! I hungered for God, and He manifested blessings to me. Then I met a full-gospel pastor, and he invited me to a Full Gospel Business Men's Fellowship International (FGBMFI) meeting.

I did not really want to go, but finally this rich man came to town to speak at one of their meetings, so I went. He began talking about speaking in tongues and receiving power from on high. I could not believe what he said.

He said, "In my department store, I have a special chair in my office where I pray for people." He would look out over his customers, and God would show him someone who

24

was dying. Then he would take that person into his office, have him sit in that chair, and pray for him (or her).

I had not even seen this happen in church!

I thought, "Jesus, You heal people in offices?"

Then this man said he did not have the power to do this until he got baptized in the Holy Spirit and started speaking in other tongues. So I began looking in his mouth for other tongues. Being a businessman, I always trained people to really listen to the words other people said. I was very sensitive to the meanings of words, and I had never heard of a human being having more than one tongue in my life.

I was ignorant, but I became interested. The next speaker at that meeting sounded like the first one.

After about a year, I received the baptism myself. I received power and got so hungry to see a miracle, but I never saw Jesus heal one person. I did not see a physical miracle. I knew there were miracles in the Bible. I was so hungry to see one.

One day, I was in Columbus, Ohio, visiting Bill Swad, who had a car dealership and talked about Jesus. I got to his car lot and began to talk to a Christian there. This man said his church had just finished a good revival. He told me of an incident that happened the first night of the revival.

The preacher was praying behind the pulpit. When he got up off his knees, he said to the congregation: "There is a man here tonight who has had an operation on his hand. I want you to stand up and stretch your hand up here toward me."

A man stood up, who had a cast on his hand. All the ligaments had been taken out. When the man stretched out his hand, the preacher said, "In Jesus' name, be healed." And the man's withered hand became normal. He began to wiggle his fingers, then he took off the cast. His hand was normal!

Doctors had told the man he would never use that hand again, and everyone in the service saw that his hand was perfectly normal. It looked just like his other hand.

I could hardly believe it, and I asked, "You mean that happened in church? What is his name? Who was the man holding the revival?"

Of course, I had never heard of the gifts of the Holy Spirit operating in our day. I had never heard of a word of knowledge.

The man talking to me said, "Lester Sumrall. He is from South Bend, Indiana."

I wrote down the name. I wanted to meet that evangelist! But I asked the man again if that really happened in church. I had been in church all my life, and I had heard about Jesus. Why had I not seen things like this happen? I had no earthly idea God did that kind of thing in churches, although I knew He had done such things in Bible days.

Then I wanted Dr. Sumrall to come to the small full-gospel church in Cleveland, Tennessee, which I was now attending. My pastor kept telling me to take it easy, and I kept saying that I could not take it easy. I wanted to see a miracle so badly!

The pastor said, "Lester Sumrall has a large ministry. He's not going to come to such a small church as this. We can't pay him what he should get."

Then I asked that, *if* Dr. Sumrall would come, could he use the church, and the pastor said yes. So I called Dr. Sumrall and told him I had been a member of a denominational church, but now I was baptized in the Holy Spirit and attending a full-gospel church. I told him I had never seen God perform a miracle and asked him to please come to Cleveland.

He said, "Well, let me check my schedule book and see." Then he came back to the phone and said, "I don't see why not."

I told my pastor that on a certain day Lester Sumrall will come to our church. It is amazing what you can get done when you have no sense. When you are determined, it is amazing what God will do for you. From the time Dr. Sumrall came to that little church, he and I have been friends. And I began to go to his meetings all over the country.

During the meetings, Dr. Sumrall came to my house for refreshments and told me he was going to Hollywood soon to be on a talk show. He asked if I would come out and be on the show with him.

My First Incident of Deliverance

So, not too long after I met him, I went to Hollywood and went on this show with him. The man introduced Dr. Sumrall as a man who went around the country casting out devils. This television host was not as genial and nice as Johnny Carson.

He said, "So, Lester, you go around casting demons out of people?"

Dr. Sumrall said, "I do if it is necessary. I do when I find them."

Then the man asked him what kind of devil he had, and Dr. Sumrall said, "I don't have any idea. Ask your wife. She'll know."

But after the show, I asked Dr. Sumrall what the Lord had shown him about the host, and he said God showed him the man was his own god, and he would get swallowed up by life and the devil. And that is what happened. He was very famous at the time, but few people would know his name now.

After that, Dr. Sumrall asked me to come to San Bernadino, California, to his next meeting. He asked me as a businessman to tell what Jesus meant to me. I agreed, and at the first service, I spoke to the people about what Jesus means to a businessman.

The greatest sermon you will ever preach is simply telling people what Jesus has done for you. As I walked off the stage and behind the curtain, the Spirit of God came over me and said, "Don't leave this meeting!" He said that in no uncertain terms.

Every Christian who wants to do something for God needs to be trained by someone already in the ministry. That is why the Apostle Paul would take different young men with him on missionary journeys. He was training them. You have to learn from someone who knows.

So I told Dr. Sumrall that I would stay and assist him in anything he wanted me to do. He told me to stay and enjoy myself and to help his sister and her husband with the book table. I went to every service and enjoyed it. After each service, the Lord would tell me not to leave yet.

Then, on the third day, at the end of the morning service, the Spirit of God came on me, and God began to bless me. Just then, Dr. Sumrall gave an invitation. I stood up, and a woman came walking up to me.

She said, "I believe you men are men of God. Every time I come to town, something goes wrong with me. I can't see it, but there are pains in my body. This thing hits me, and I just can't do anything but go home, pray, and read the Bible. Then it finally goes away. And this doesn't happen again until I go downtown the next time. I want you to pray for me."

I felt the Spirit of God on me, and I laid hands on her to pray. But the moment my hands touched hers, she jumped back, looked at me, and began to scream and growl. She looked like she wanted to fight. She looked as if she were going to attack me. But we were in church, so I knew she would not do anything. (That's all I knew!)

I looked around at the congregation, and hundreds of eyes were staring at me. Then, all of a sudden, that woman began clawing at me. I reached out and got hold of her wrists to keep from being beat up in church, and I thought, "She's crazy."

Then she fell on the floor, flat on her back. About that time, I heard a loud, strong voice calling, "Cast that thing out of her!"

I looked up at the platform, and Dr. Sumrall was standing there relaxed, leaning on the pulpit. By now I was a nervous wreck.

I said, "Yeah, okay," but I was thinking, "What thing? Cast what thing out of her?"

Then Dr. Sumrall said, "And don't let her talk either!"

I looked at her, then at the congregation staring at me and waiting to see what I was going to do.

My mind said, "What do I do? Smack her in the mouth? You can't stop her talking."

Dr. Sumrall's brother-in-law, the Rev. James Murphy, jumped up and came over to me. Thank God for him! He got hold of the woman and cast the devil out of her.

He said, "In Jesus' name, you listen to me and come out of her!"

And I said, "Yeah!" as if I knew what he was doing. Of course, I did not know what to do or say. But he looked as if he knew what he was doing, so I echoed him.

All of a sudden, the woman went as limp as if we had killed her. I had seen Westerns as a kid where the characters who were shot did that, and I was just sure we had killed her. I had never seen anyone outside the movies fall like that. So I stepped back a few steps, not knowing what to do.

In about sixty seconds, I saw a woman turn from a devil to an angel. I saw tears running down her cheek, and I heard her sniffle. Pretty soon, I could hear her thanking Jesus in a real sweet angelic voice. She had a glow about her. Now she looked beautiful. We helped her up, and she was getting blessed and more blessed by the Lord.

All of a sudden, the Lord told me I could leave the meeting now and go home.

The next week as I rode around checking on my businesses, the Spirit of the Lord fell on me and told me to go study Mark 16 right that minute. I hurried home, grabbed my Bible, and began to read. Jesus told me verses 15-18 contained the greatest words that ever came out of His mouth.

That is how I began to learn about casting out demons.

4

The Devil Must Obey You

If you stand on God's Word in the name of Jesus, the devil *has* to obey you. The only reason he does not is that you waver in your faith. The devil never has to obey someone who wavers. The Bible says that one who wavers will not receive from God. (James 1:6-8.) Of course, he does not want to obey, so he looks for every little excuse not to obey. However, Jesus gave us all power and authority over demons and diseases. (Luke 9:1.)

You even have the power through the Holy Spirit inside you to take authority over any demonic influence on you. I am not talking about possession, but oppression. Many people stay oppressed all their lives and never get totally possessed.

However, the way to become possessed is to enter into temptation and stay involved in whatever sin that means.

What does *oppression* mean? Demonic influence takes the form of such things as fear, nervousness, depression, rejection, self-pity, and so forth. *You can keep a relationship with God and still be oppressed by demons.*

If you do fall into some kind of temptation, repent immediately and ask for forgiveness. If you believe the Word and walk in faith without wavering, the Holy Spirit will empower you for victorious living.

The kind of faith that does not waver and will get your prayers answered is the kind the wife of a surgeon in Florida has. Evangelist Kenneth Copeland tells of visiting this man and his wife. Kenneth and his wife, Gloria, had been invited for supper after a service.

However, their hostess had gotten busy and forgotten to buy the steaks for the meal she had planned. When Ken and Gloria got there after the service, it was about 11 p.m. He said they talked for a while, and he did not see any food anywhere.

Then the lady said, "Brother Copeland, you know the faith you preach about? You had better put it to work if you want to eat. I am thanking God for sending steaks to us. How about you, Ken? It is believe God or nothing."

[This couple also are friends of Dr. Kenneth Hagin's, and he says this lady operates this way all of the time.]

About that time, someone rang the doorbell. She walked over and opened the door, and there sat a box.

She said, "Oh, thank You, Lord, for the steaks," brought the box in and opened it up. Inside was a box full of the biggest, prettiest steaks you have ever seen.

Authority has to be exercised in faith to work.

Having the Wisdom of Christ

If you want the Lord to lead you, you must have the wisdom of God and the mind of Christ. Every case of demonic influence, oppression, or possession is different. Authority has to be exercised for different situations in different ways.

A thirteen-year-old boy was brought to me once. A friend of mine knew this boy's family and the trouble he was in and thought I might be able to help. So they came and visited me. No school would allow the boy to attend, because he kept trying to burn down the school buildings. Demonic power drove him to set the schools on fire, and children could have been killed.

You cannot begin to tell a thirteen-year-old who does not know much about God that demons are running his life. When I met this boy, he seemed to be one of the nicest boys you would ever meet. He was well-mannered, and his parents were really nice people. So I prayed for favor with him. I prayed for him to be able to trust me.

We had lunch out, and I had him sit next to me. I was spending time trying to get acquainted with him. I just talked to him off and on about different subjects, but also, I talked to his parents casually. I wanted to put no pressure on him or on the demon.

Then I said, "Let's go over, and I'll show you the church."

After that, I took him back to my office to talk. Then the Holy Spirit gave me words to relate to him. I began to tell him of things I had done as a child, things I could not tell my father. I told him of things that just happened, and how I could not seem to stop myself.

Then a strange look came over his face, and he said, "I just had to set the schools on fire. I just had to do it. I just *had* to do it."

I just kept talking. I knew the power and authority was within me to cast out that demon who was trying to put this boy in prison for the rest of his life after causing much pain and heartache for the parents.

I told him that I understood what he was going through. I told him when I was a boy, I knew it was wrong to get down in a ditch and smoke cigarettes, but I did it anyway.

Then I said, "I'll bet you wish that power wouldn't come over you."

He said, "Oh, yeah! I wish I didn't have to do it. I wish I didn't have to set schools on fire."

Then I asked him if he knew Jesus loves us so much He will do anything for us.

I said, "Let's just pray in Jesus' name and bind up all the powers that try to destroy us."

He agreed, so I laid hands on him and cast out that demon in Jesus' name. I told that demon I would not let him drive this boy into anything again. I bound that demon up and commanded him to go from the boy "right now, in Jesus' name."

I said, "I have power over you, in Jesus' name."

The demon left, and the boy was free of that pyromaniacal compulsion.

You need to recognize that, as a child of God, you have power and authority over all devils. You have to recognize that. You have to know that. In God, there is no wondering. You either know, or you do not know.

God is saying, "I gave you My Son's name, the name of the Head of the Church, and the gates of hell cannot prevail against that name."

The truth is that every sick, oppressed, demon-possessed person who walks into a church building ought to be set free. There is power available to do that, if you believe it and operate in it. You have the power and authority.

The most important thing is to love the Lord, to worship and praise Him. But you also must know that you have power over devils in you. The Holy Spirit stays ready to move when you allow Him to. Take authority over devils. The name of Jesus is more powerful than all devils.

The Power of Jesus' Name

Once, a lady came to see me about her husband. He would not leave the bedroom, but he wanted to rule the house. I went to visit them. When I opened the door to the bedroom, I found a businessman sitting in the middle of the bed, dressed in a suit and holding a yardstick.

He was sitting in a dark room with sun shades on humming to himself. He had not been out of the room in five years. A Bible was laying on the bed, and he said it was a good book.

The devil will say the Bible is a good book, but he does not read it.

Finally, we got the man out of bed, but when he got close to the door, he would say he had better not go out of there.

He said, "I have to stay in here. I'll die if I go out there."

He had gotten sick once, and the doctor had told him to stay in for a while. A demon dropped down on him and began to tell him that he was sick and would die if he went outside. The demon had told him that so many times that he really believed it.

Doctors would come and tell him he was well, and he would not believe them. A demon bound this man in his own house.

When you are dealing in deliverance, pray for wisdom over everything a demon has told a person to do. Then get that person to do the opposite. The devil is not nearly as strong as he thinks he is. Compared to you and the Holy Spirit, the devil is not strong at all.

I told the people with us that the man would fight us because the devil had controlled him for five years. I told them we had to make the man go outside, no matter what we had to do to accomplish that.

I said, "We'll throw him outside, but he will fight us, so be ready. We can't pray for him yet because he won't listen."

Faith involves patience. There is nothing God will not do for you or tell you how to do, if you can keep from getting shook up about it. We need to just pray and ask God what to do. That is what prayer is for.

The man's uncle asked him to come into the hall to see something and talk. Finally, he made a few steps down the hallway. We kind of circled around him as if we were not going to do a thing.

Then I said, "In Jesus' name!" and we threw him out the door. We literally bodily dragged him outside.

He was crying, "I'll die. I'll die."

I said, "Oh, shut up! You're not going to die."

We broke the power of the devil over him in Jesus' name.

Then his wife came running out telling us to stop before he had a heart attack. I wanted to tell her to shut up! But we turned him loose, and he took off back in the house fast and sat down panting for breath.

In a few minutes, we walked back in and confessed his freedom in the name of Jesus.

All of a sudden, he said, "I didn't die, did I?"

"No," I said. "You're free, not dead."

He said, "I went outside and saw the sky where the sun was shining, and I didn't die."

"No," I said, "you're alive, and you can be outside and go to work. You are free."

In a couple of days, he went back outside. Then he began to go to work every day running his car dealership as he used to do. Those devils had made him a slave in his own house and eventually would have killed him. He would have gone completely crazy in about another year. But Jesus gave us power and authority over all devils.

Do Not Put Up With Pain

I was holding a meeting in Alabama one day, when a car pulled into the church parking lot. A man came running in looking for the pastor. There was a woman in town screaming in pain. We went to her house.

We walked into the bedroom where she was screaming in pain. I said, "In Jesus' name, I don't put up with pain." Then I walked through the house saying, "In Jesus' name, she is free."

I jumped up on the bed with the woman, grabbed her, and said five or six times, "Come out of her, pain, in Jesus' name."

Then she fell over as if she had died, and the glory of the Lord came into the room. I got off the bed and told her husband that she was healed and that she was now free from pain. I told him she would be okay from now on.

He said, "What church did you say you were from?"

I explained that I was visiting town preaching at the church where he had come for help. That night they were at the services. When people see the beauty and power of Jesus' name, they are hungry for it.

I wanted God to touch my mind, to help me think straight. Three years, I prayed that prayer — three years! Then one day, I heard Kenneth E. Hagin teach the Bible, and the Spirit of God just came on me. He began to talk to me and touch my mind. I let the Word go into my mind and into my spirit.

I have not had a confused day in years. I have the peace of God in my mind. I do not have confused days the way I used to do. It is hell on earth to have a confused mind. But when the Lord touches your mind, you are free.

When the devil comes to attempt to mess up your mind, just say, "No, you don't!"

Tell him exactly what to do, and he will obey you. But you must tell him with authority. Don't let the devil say you do not have the power to cast him out.

Take authority over disease and stop it yourself. The devil will attack everything you have, if you keep telling the truth.

Brother Hagin was visiting me once, and we went to a neighbor's house, a denominational family, for dinner. My sixteen-year-old daughter walked in. She was in high school, and she had knots all over her. She had the worst looking hands I had ever seen on a girl. There were forty-two knots and warts on her. She had them for three years.

At that time, I already had studied the Bible on the subject of faith for years. I thought I knew what faith meant until I ran into knots and warts. Then I found I did not know as much as I thought I did.

I knew the devil had put those things on my daughter's body, but I did not know what to do about them.

Brother Hagin said, "How are you doing, Zona?"

She said, "I'm fine, but it's my dad. You need to talk to him. I've been trying to get him to take me to the hospital to have these stupid warts taken off. Look at me! My hands look awful, but he won't take me. He just keeps telling me, 'Well, we'll see, Honey.'"

Dr. Hagin said, "I can curse those things and make them disappear."

I believed him, but I looked over at this woman in whose house we were, and I could see that his words did not go over big in a denominational home. I wanted to ask him how he would do that, but I did not. Then for several days, I wondered why I did not ask. I realized God wants us to be able to do that ourselves.

The devil may go around your town messing up other people, but that is no sign he has to do it to you. If you parents do not know any better, you will have to put up with the devil. He will come after your children. It was my own dumb fault that my daughter had those awful warts on her body for all those years.

I got mad at myself and told God I wanted to know the truth. I found out something about God. When you get desperate to know the truth, the Lord will give it to you. He will teach you. The Holy Spirit inside of you is the teacher. If you listen, He will teach you all of the truth.

I sought God for two weeks, and suddenly, He began to talk to me. I could hear Him talk to me in plain words.

He said, "How long are you going to put up with those things on your daughter's body? Those are the works of the devil."

Let me show you something I learned at that point. Jesus will put up with anything as long as you will. You must make an effort and take a step toward Him. Your faith must have some kind of action involved. You must press in on God. When God talks to me, such a holy awe comes on me, I get afraid.

I said, "I don't know how long."

My ignorance made Him mad. Doubt makes God get stern with you, and He blasted me.

He said, "You're the head of this house. You are the head of your house. If you go in there and curse those things in My name, they will die and disappear."

Then I was reminded of Brother Hagin's words. I had to do it myself. Brother Hagin does not have the time to go to everyone's house. We must learn to walk in the power and authority of Jesus' name ourselves.

You have the right to use Jesus' name just as I did. When the Lord told me that, I went right into my daughter's room and cursed those warts. I commanded them to disappear, and in thirty days, they were all gone.

One day, she was hanging up dresses when, all of a sudden, realized that she had brand new hands and legs. She had brand new shiny skin, and it scared her.

She came running in to me, and I saw brand new hands.

My daughter said, "I can understand God doing something for you, because you work for Him. But I don't work for Him, and He loves me enough to do this?"

Perhaps you have felt the same. God will do things like that for Norvel Hayes, but not for me. Perhaps you are saying that you are not a minister, a teacher, nor an evangelist. That does not matter. All believers were told by Jesus to cast out devils and lay hands on the sick. And He promised that if we did, the sick would recover and nothing would hurt us.

The Great Commission: Jesus' Greatest Words

Look at what we call "the Great Commission":

> And he said unto them, Go ye into all the world, and preach the gospel to every creature.
>
> He that believeth and is baptized shall be saved; but he that believeth not shall be damned.
>
> And these signs shall follow them that believe; In my name shall they cast out devils; they shall speak with new tongues;
>
> They shall take up serpents; and if they drink any deadly thing, it shall not hurt them; they shall lay hands on the sick, and they shall recover.
>
> **Mark 16:15-18**

The first thing Jesus told believers to do was preach the Gospel to every creature, and right after that, His instruction was to *cast out devils*. That is how important dealing with the enemy is to the Lord.

Even if you are not called to public ministry, you can cast out devils. Do it in your own home, when the devil comes to steal, kill, or destroy. And do not talk to the devil easy. He never listens to weak people. You have to speak strongly and use the name of Jesus. If you do not know how, it is your responsibility to learn, just as it is your responsibility to witness to others of Jesus.

One time at a church service, the pastor asked me to pray for this young girl. She was full of demons, but I did not know that. She was a college student, who had been with a lot of boys. We prayed, and she asked Satan to leave her in a very weak voice.

I got her to speak up and tell the devil in strong words to release her and to leave her, and the demons did.

Several months later, her pastor called, and this girl had met a nice young man. They were to be married, and they wanted me to read the Bible at the wedding ceremony. I agreed to do that.

During the wedding, as she was walking down the aisle toward the altar, I heard the Lord speak loud and clear to me.

He said, "Thank you for obeying the sixteenth chapter of the book of Mark. Thank you for obeying the Bible, for praying for that girl and setting her free. She stands before Me now as clean and pure as an angel of heaven."

The Lord thanked me for obeying the Bible so that He could manifest Himself.

5
The Power of Praying in the Spirit

I was in a missionary meeting once with about seven people in a college Campus Challenge team. When I finished speaking, the Lord told me to pray in the Spirit. When you pray in the Spirit, the Holy Spirit can do so much that our minds do not understand.

After about twenty minutes of praying in the Spirit, a woman stood up and began to shout and rejoice. After she calmed down, she said her daughter was a missionary overseas to a tribe of people. The daughter had a disease and was dying. The demons attached to that tribe were killing her. The doctors said there was nothing they could do to heal her. She had no hope at all.

The woman said that while I was praying in tongues, all of a sudden, some of the words were the language spoken by that tribe.

She said, "You just claimed healing over my daughter. When you did that, the Lord showed me that all those demons left my daughter, and she is free!"

Praying in the Spirit can make devils leave. God's power is strong, if you will pray in the Spirit. Sometimes you will not even know what is going on. I did not know what I was speaking. I had no earthly idea what I was praying for.

The things you cannot figure out, call out to God and pray in tongues. The Spirit of God knows how to get victory in every case. If you will let Him come through you and pray in tongues, He knows the will of God in every situation.

Once I got a phone call from Indiana inviting me to hold a meeting. I agreed and went to that town to hold a meeting in a motel ballroom. The last night, I spoke on God's power for deliverance and healing in the laying on of hands. After the sermon, I gave the invitation, and this girl who had been crippled for years came to the front.

She fell backwards onto the floor under the power of the Holy Spirit, and I kept going on to other people. In just a minute, she got up and went back to her seat, leaving her crutches on the floor.

God Operates in Different Ways

Another way God operates is simply to have you speak to diseases, and they will disappear. This has only happened to me a few times.

That night in Indiana, I walked up to the first person in line and said, "In Jesus' name, disease, die!"

Then I did it to the next one and the next one, never touching them, only speaking the command of the Lord. After the last one in line, the Lord told me there was a demon-possessed woman in the congregation.

He said, "What are you going to do about it?"

I knew who she was and where she was, so I obeyed Mark 16. God is always wanting you to show Him something. Tell Him you are going to do something, and He will say, "Show Me."

Also, your soul is saved, but your body is not. Tell it to shut up when it wants things such as cigarettes, drugs, alcohol. You must *show* God that you will quit smoking for Him, show Him you will win sinners to Him.

When I was young and people came to visit us, I had to address them as "sir" or "ma'am," or I would get a piece of the peach tree used on my legs. When you are taught like that, you learn how to use your mouth.

What would you do if a totally demon-possessed woman was in the room with you, and you knew it?

Well, that night, I calmly walked out into the congregation. When I got a few feet away from her, I pointed my finger at her.

I said, "In the name of the Lord Jesus Christ, I am not going to let you have that woman. Now you get out of her."

She got out of her seat. Devils are bold, you know. She stood up, stuck out her chest, and that thing in her said, "In Lucifer's name, I won't come out."

Right in a church service, the demon said that. And that whole Indiana ballroom full of Christians went "Ooooooh!"

I said, "Yes, you *will* come out, because Jesus sent me to her to do this, and Jesus is stronger than you are."

She tried to get away, but I just grabbed her and said, "Come out of her!"

Then the Lord suddenly said, "Call forty people to come pray in tongues right now!"

Those Hoosiers believed every word I said. They jumped up and got around her and began to pray in tongues as hard and fast as they could. I had already broken the power of that demon, and as they prayed, the woman just screamed and screamed, lying on the floor.

After a while, the hotel manager came in and said in a wimpy voice, "What's going on?"

I said, "Nothing much, sir. We're just praying for a lady over here."

Midnight came, and we were still there. Then the pastor of a large church in the area came up and asked me to preach the next morning and evening at his church.

"But," he said, "I don't believe in people falling down," he said.

He had seen people being "slain in the Spirit" all evening, but he still did not believe it. But he had to ask me to come to his church the next day because the Lord told him to.

He said, "Sunday morning, just preach, and then turn the service over to me. Then Sunday night you can do what you want."

Sunday evening, no one in the healing line was slain in the Spirit. But you always get in church what you believe. Then all of a sudden, a woman came up and said she had not wanted to come up before, but Jesus wanted me to pray for her. As soon as I began to pray for the lady, she fell back on the floor. Guess who it was? You are right — the pastor's wife!

She had been a Satan-worshipper, and she said, "Demons have been whipping me every time I go to church lately. Once I drank some human blood from someone the coven I was in had killed. But then they told me I had to kill a human child and drink its blood there in front of all of them. When I would not do it, they started whipping me."

Jesus loved that woman as much as He loves any of the rest of us. I found out later that thirty-five Spirit-filled women had been praying for that woman.

You can never back away from the devil. The best thing is to learn to be patient in the Spirit. Jesus' name is stronger than all devils. But when you run into someone who literally has been worshipping them, they do not come out so easily.

You cannot make all of them leave real quickly. Some are strong, and you do not know how to do everything. But the Spirit of God knows how. And no matter how much experience you have, you will still run into cases that you do not know how to pray for. So use the Word of God and pray in the Holy Spirit. The Holy Spirit knows exactly what to do in every case.

The Spirit of God knows how to get freedom for everyone. He confirms the Word with signs following.

> **Likewise the Spirit also helpeth our infirmities: for we know not what we should pray for as we ought: but the Spirit itself maketh intercession for us with groanings which cannot be uttered.**
>
> **And he that searcheth the hearts knoweth what is the mind of the Spirit, because he maketh intercession for the saints according to the will of God.**
>
> Romans 8:26,27

For that demon-possessed woman, the will of God was freedom. The devil wants humans to worship him. However, the will of God is for everyone to be free from demons and to be able to worship Him. Getting that woman free took four hours of praying in the Spirit.

The Holy Spirit knew exactly what to do. I did my part. I spoke to the demons and told them to get out of her. The Spirit knows the rest. He will get the demons out and bring deliverance. The will of God is freedom for everyone.

Learn From Someone Who Knows How

God called me in the early Seventies to start a Bible school. I have the students watch me cast out demons. That is how they learn. Also, we have counseling sessions that they sit in on.

One such incident that they learned from was the time a Pentecostal preacher brought a young man and his mother to me. He was breaking into people's houses and stealing women's underwear. His mother was Spirit-filled, but she could not do anything with him.

He would take women's panties and hang them on trees and lights, and so forth.

I said, "If you will do what I tell you, I'll bind that demon up. And I'll teach you how to bind demons yourself. You can walk out of this office free. Devils are crazy."

He said, "Mr. Hayes, some kind of power comes on me and drives me to do that."

I said, "I understand, and I'm going to break that power."

Just the day before, they had been working at the church when suddenly the boy excused himself and never came back. I found later that he had broken into someone's house and hung panties everywhere.

I prayed for the young man, bound up, and broke the power of the devil over him. I made the devil leave him in the name of Jesus and taught him how to resist the devil.

I said to him, "Every time that supernatural power comes on you and tries to make you steal women's underwear, that demon is manifesting itself through the power of the devil.

"Quickly say, 'In Jesus' name, I resist you. I bind you, Satan. In Jesus' name, go from me!'

"Do this eight to twelve times, loud and strong.

"Then raise your hands and worship the Lord, saying, 'I am strong in the Lord, not weak.'

"The urge for wrong will disappear. Each time, do the same thing. Don't look for something new."

In a case like this, I knew that if he did not get the truth in him, the devil would destroy him. Human beings are God's pride of creation, and the devil loves to hurt God by taking over one of His creatures and taking them to hell. God does not want us getting messed up by demons.

However, you do not need to get focused on demons and look for them behind every bush (although there is probably one there). But focus on Jesus and be obedient to His commands. You are casting out demons for His benefit, as part of occupying the territory He bought back with His precious blood.

Devils will never get into you, if you refuse to participate with them and do not yield to their temptations. Hanging around the wrong people will lead you into temptation. Attending services in a dry church will make you dry ground and good soil for demonic influence, but not for the Word.

Feed yourself with the Word and pray in tongues. Put on the whole armor of God. (Eph. 6:11-18.)

Dry church services many times take place in beautiful buildings and have beautiful music. The services are soothing to your soul, but your spirit goes hungry. The first few services, you know better. Perhaps you can hardly stand it. But then you begin to get used to it. Finally, you like those kinds of services.

Falling into other kinds of temptations, even into carnal sins, follows the same pattern. Withstand the wiles of the enemy, and you will not be oppressed by Satan.

A Foundation of Faith, Power, and Authority

Once I was ministering to a young lady and told her about my daughter's healing. Now, I did not know it, but this young lady was a prostitute. As I talked, the Spirit of God gave me the words to say to her. I told her of how an angel had visited my daughter, and she did not know what an angel was.

When I told her, she began to weep and ran down the hall to the ladies' room. I sent two girls to bring her back, and when she returned, I backed her up against the wall and cast demons out of her. This was in a hotel, and she had been working in the bar. I cast the demons out of her right in front of the bar.

I told her that if she would let me, I would help her get to heaven. The next day, she brought a friend who was a prostitute, and she also became born again.

While I was in my room, still staying in that hotel for that particular meeting, the Lord spoke to me to take those two ex-prostitutes with me when I left town. So I told them to pack all their clothes and be ready to leave on Sunday morning. I told them that the Lord did not want them to stay there.

When they showed up ready to leave on Sunday morning, they had their clothes in garbage bags. The devil had lied to them. He had told them prostitution was a way to make good money, but they had ended up without a thing.

So the girls went with me to my next meeting where the Lord instructed me to tell the congregation their story. When I got through, the people there began to come down to the altar and pile up money for those girls. God does things up big!

The first girl went to work for my ministry, and the other girl was trained as a team leader. When you set people free in Jesus' name, they always have a deep love for you the rest of their lives.

Mark 16:9 says that, when Jesus rose from the dead, He appeared first to Mary Magdalene out of whom He had cast seven devils. I think He appeared to her first because she loved Him the most. If God cannot get Christians to teach the Gospel, He will get people like that prostitute to do it. He will use anyone who will be available.

6

Dealing With Satan Through Faith

There is a lot more to casting out devils than just casting them out. Faith has a lot to do with dealing with the devil. In fact, faith is the number-one thing. Your faith in God has a lot to do with how you take authority over devils. You have to learn that faith comes first.

You must totally, completely walk in faith. You must stand up to the devil and refuse to waver. The longer you pray, the stronger you get. The devil never obeys weak people. Never. He only obeys authority, in the name of Jesus.

When an alcoholic demon has been in a person for years, he will not come out quickly. You must absolutely take authority over him. Speaking in Jesus' name, you can make that demon do anything. You cannot ask him to do anything. You must *make* him obey. So many people do not believe in the power of faith.

If that person harboring an alcoholic demon wants to stay an alcoholic, there is nothing you can do. But if he wants to change, it can be done.

Homosexual demons are one of the hardest kinds to get rid of. Most I have dealt with have been in the men since they were little boys. So you parents of little boys, watch out who your children spend the night with. Someone might get hold of him, and in fifteen years, that will be the only thing they know.

Everything that God has that is beautiful and sweet for you, the devil wants — but he wants it warped, perverted in some way. But the devil tells churches all over the world to read the Bible and make up their own doctrines. He has stolen God's Word away from so many churches.

The Lord told us in the Great Commission to do four things: preach the Gospel, cast out devils, speak in new tongues, and lay hands on sick people who will recover. (Mark 16:15-18.) Yet there are many, many churches that build great buildings, carry on a multitude of activities, hold revival services, and do not do any of those four things.

No one in those churches has enough power to get an alcoholic demon out of a man. Even full-gospel people give up too quickly.

Do Not Give Up Too Quickly

Thirty minutes of praying, and they say, "Well, I guess God doesn't want him healed or delivered."

Wrong! If that person wants to be free, and you do not get him free, it means your faith is not strong enough or your faith does not possess patience. The key to the whole thing is that faith must include patience.

If you pray for someone and nothing happens, pray longer. Deal with people in love at first. Then if the demons will not be quiet, take the person out to a smaller room. But if a demon acts up really badly, just jump on him. Let him know he is in the Lord's house, and you will not put up with junk like that.

Start out softly, but remember that some devils are very strong. You are still dealing with the demonic attitude that tried to take over heaven. Demons will try to take over the service. I had a woman come into my service once who did that.

Her daughters had brought her to the service, and about halfway through, she began calling me a profane name and walking around. I called to her to come down to the front and called the demon out of her. She kept calling me names, but we finally broke the devil's power over her.

Every time she spoke, I said, "Oh, shut up! You come out of her."

I stood up there as if I had some sense. You are not supposed to get nervous about the devil. God does not answer prayers of nervous faith. If you want strong faith, you must obey Mark 11:23:

> For verily I say unto you, That whosoever shall say unto this mountain, Be thou removed, and be thou cast into the sea; and shall not doubt in his heart, but shall believe that those things which he saith shall come to pass; he shall have whatsoever he saith.

Begin to say, "My spirit possesses patience. My mind, in Jesus' name, is quiet and settled on Jesus once and for all. I think the way the Lord thinks. I have the patience of Job and of God, and I have faith. Patience is mine, in Jesus' name."

Repeat that, believing, for four or five days, and patience will develop in you. From then on, spend time praying in tongues each day, and your nervous days will be over. I do not have any nervous, upset days anymore. I just rest in God and enjoy myself. I can be satisfied anywhere. I can eat steak, or I can eat hot dogs.

Resist Temptation

If I did not disappear after the services at Dr. Kenneth E. Hagin's annual summer campmeetings in Tulsa, Oklahoma, I would be doing nothing but casting out devils. One year, a man sat at the door every day until he caught me. He was from Omaha, Nebraska, and the only reason he came to campmeeting was to see me and get delivered.

He said that he was demon possessed. He told me some of the bad things he wanted to do to women. And he wanted me to cast that thing out of him.

I said, "Have you ever done any of those things?"

He said, "Oh, no. I've never done any of them."

I wanted to grab him and smack him, but I did not, because I am a nice guy.

I said, "You're not demon possessed. That is only temptation. But you have been listening to a dumb demon. Next time he approaches you, just say, 'In the name of Jesus, you stupid demon, go!' "

That young man had never obeyed the devil. But if he had kept listening to that demon for a year or two, he would have given in to what it said. Probably, he would have broken the law, hurt people, and ended up in prison. Resist the devil, and he will flee from you. First of all, submit yourself to God. Get on your knees and pray, worship the Lord, tell Him you love Him. Then resist the devil, and he will flee from you.

There are certain things you must do to stay strong: raise your hands and praise the Lord, read the Bible, worship the Lord, pray. If you are going to be a warrior and a servant of God, you cannot go around doing your own thing.

> **My brethren, count it all joy when ye fall into divers temptations.**
>
> **Knowing this, that the trying of your faith worketh patience.**
>
> **But let patience have her perfect work, that ye may be perfect and entire, wanting nothing.**
>
> **James 1:2-4**

The kind of faith that Abraham had can get you what you want from heaven. God can use you to minister to others, and you will be a blessing to many. He will give you orders of certain things to do. And, if you are obedient, you will be blessed.

Orders From God

> **By faith Abraham, when he was tried, offered up Isaac: and he that had received the promises offered up his only begotten son,**

> Of whom it was said, That in Isaac shall thy seed be called:

> Accounting that God was able to raise him up, even from the dead; from whence also he received him in a figure.
> Hebrews 11:17-19

Years ago, a young man walked into one of Lester Sumrall's services in Chattanooga, Tennessee. He had tattoos all over his arms, a black bag tied to each arm, and a tooth hanging around his neck. He was wearing tight jeans and a sleeveless T-shirt. He walked right up to the altar and said "something" told him to come in. He was a hippie cult leader from Nashville.

He said, "Something's been playing tricks on my mind. I was on my way to Florida to get acid, and my truck broke down up on the interstate. Something told me to come in here. Something spoke to my mind."

I said, "Yes, it was God. That's for sure."

Lester Sumrall and I began ministering to the young man, and when we said, "In Jesus' name, come out of him," that thing came out. He began to cry and said, "I didn't know God loved me."

Thirty minutes later, he was still saying the same thing: "I didn't know God loved me."

He had been in prison twice and had been going across the country making a living by robbing different places. No one had ever told him that he loved him. He wept and wept and became so bold for God. He even told the policeman by his broken-down vehicle that God had got the demons out of him and that he had not known before that God loved him.

Newspaper and television reporters found out about the incident, and he got a lot of coverage in the media.

During a television interview, he told exactly what had happened and how he had discovered that God loved him.

I had never seen anything like it in my life. We decided not to close the meeting. Dr. Sumrall went home to Indiana, but I continued for three more days.

During one of those nights, television cameramen and local television stars showed up to see what was going on. By the end of the service, they were crying. God saved so many people that we had to buy a house there where young people could come, and we left this young former hippie in charge of it.

The Body Affects the Mind

Some time later, I was in my hometown of Cleveland, Tennesse, when the Lord spoke to me and gave me orders to go to that house in Chattanooga immediately. I did, and when I got there, this young man ran out onto the driveway to meet my car.

He had shaved, cut his hair, and was wearing long-sleeved shirts to cover up the tattoos.

He said, "God sent you, didn't He? There is a crazy boy in the house."

We went inside, and there were two very distinguished-looking men, one of them a doctor, and a college student. A few days before this young man's mind had snapped. He was "streaking" (running nude) across campus, and he had been totally out of his mind ever since. He did not even know his own name.

What you do with your body affects your mind. (I discuss this in more depth in Chapter 9.) As long as you live, this will be true. All the demons or foul spirits cannot drive you crazy if you keep your body clean. Devils are such liars! But when you have worked with as many oppressed people as I have, you know that the human mind cannot "go crazy" unless a person has been involved in an accident that has damaged the mind or brain, or has participated in abnormal sex acts or had addictions or compulsions — some misuse of the body.

I have visited people in mental institutions many times, and every one of them had done something with their bodies that had resulted in addictions, perversions, or compulsions.

To keep your mind full of peace and joy, do not get involved in abnormal sex acts. Keep everything normal between a husband and wife, even. The cleaner you keep your sex life, the more peace of mind you will have. *What you do with your body affects your mind.*

Many times, the things that happened with the bodies began at a very young age. Satan cannot drive you mentally insane if you do not give him the power.

Do not ever say you are afraid of the devil. You will wind up oppressed, if you do that. He will take advantage of your fear to come visit you. But when he comes to tempt you with anything — even fear — do not listen to him.

The doctor with this college student said, "A year ago, I did not believe in demons or deliverance. But I saw this man on television, and he was so sincere and described demon possession so well that I have to agree that this student is demon possessed. Would you be willing to minister to him?"

I said, "I will, if you fellows will leave me alone. I cannot have you in the room, because you do not know enough about it. I cannot have unbelief in the room."

We walked into the room where the young man was, and the doctor introduced me and then left. The boy was looking strange, staring out into space.

James 5:15 says that the prayer of faith will save the sick, and Mark 11:24 tells me to believe when I pray that I will receive. The prayer of faith is important to you in dealing with demons.

So I walked up to him, just taking my time, and laid my hands on his head.

I prayed, "Father, I claim in the name of the Lord Jesus Christ for this boy to be normal and for his mind to be restored to him."

Then I said, "Satan, I break your power deep inside of him. Turn him loose. In Jesus' name, you cannot have this boy."

Then I thanked the Lord for the victory. Something that is important to remember is not to let the devil make you nervous. Exercise your faith in patience and believe deliverance already is available for the person with whom you are dealing.

I just went over to a chair, sat down, and began to enjoy myself thanking the Lord for ten or fifteen minutes. Then I spoke to Satan again in Jesus' name, telling that demon he could not have the boy's mind. I thanked the Lord that he was free and his mind was restored. Then I rested for another fifteen minutes and started over.

How long did I sit there? Normally, I would not sit there that long, but this time I stayed all night. God had sent me, and I had no release to leave. I began to pray about 8 p.m., and I sat there until about 4 a.m.

One time, the young man got up, went across the room, lay down in the corner like a dog, and began to bark and ask for water.

The psychiatrist was in the room, and here he came with water, just like an English butler.

I said, "What are you doing? I don't obey devils. I don't give devils a drink. Now, listen, sir, I love you, but leave me alone. Don't give demons *anything* they ask for."

The longer I stayed, the louder I got. About every fifteen or twenty minutes, I would tell the devil he could not have the boy's mind.

About 4 a.m., he got up from the corner and walked across the room toward me. He stopped right in front of me and began to laugh without any sound, and he did this for about fifteen minutes. It may have looked as if nothing was happening, but I knew that when Jesus died on the cross and was raised from the dead, freedom was provided for this young man.

He began to stand on one leg and stayed that way for about forty-five minutes, then his tongue began to come out of his mouth — but it was the enemy's tongue. Then the young man's mouth came open and some white foam began to run down and puddle on the floor.

During all of this, I just stayed steadfast and kept saying the same things I had been saying for the previous eight hours. After that, the demon loosed his mind, and he came to himself. Eight hours of praying in faith and claiming by faith, and this student got his mind back.

Refuse To Let Satan Push You Around

You can do this. Refuse to take anything from the devil. Be faithful and patient in the name of Jesus Christ.

If you ever depart from having faith in doing the things that Jesus did or things He has taught you to do and begin to do things the way you want to do them, that is when you start getting into false doctrines. You would be surprised at how many churches that are basically right in the things they do and believe, *but* the things Jesus did in the supernatural and told us to do they leave out.

They tell the Gospel, but leave out casting out demons and laying hands on the sick. As long as a believer lives, it is his, or her, responsibility to lay hands on the sick and see them recover. God's power flows through people's hands. The "laying on of hands" is a doctrine of the New Covenant (Testament) Church. Faith in God is a doctrine of the Church. Without faith, it is impossible to please God. (Heb. 11:6.)

God honors determined faith. If you yield yourself to a certain type of demon, it will think you want it. If you obey it all of the time, it will not come out so easily.

Demons may growl at you, or you may not hear a thing. But make them mad, and make them get out. Sometimes it takes hours. I prayed for that one young man eight hours one night, all night long, because the Lord sent me. And do not get nervous. The Holy Spirit does not get nervous over devils. They are already defeated. Develop the patience of God if you are going to cast out devils. God does not know the meaning of defeat.

Nor does God know the meaning of poverty. When you are dealing with God, you are dealing with first-class things. There is total victory in Jesus' name. But you must have faith and learn to talk to the devil with authority. Be humble with God, compassionate with human beings, but be strong as an ox with the devil. You must have a one-track mind with the devil. You must have one goal, and that is to get that demon out of that person. Jesus came to set people free.

7

The Importance of the Word

I could teach a month on the importance of God's Word in dealing with the devil. There is no end to the goodness of God.

So many people want to give their hearts to God, but not their lives. Years ago, when I first gave my heart to God, I could not believe He wanted me to teach the Bible in public. I told God I came from a religious background, and I had no sense about the Holy Spirit's workings.

He said, "I don't care. I'm calling you to cast out devils. I'm taking all of the shame of the Gospel out of you, and you'll be free to work for Me."

So I promised Jesus that no matter where He took me, I would never stop casting out devils and praying for sick people. When I began to cast out devils, some people thought I had gone crazy. They just wanted to go to church on Sunday. They thought I was going too far.

But I never did find out what life was really about until I came into contact with Jesus. He will give you a precious life to share with Him all of the time.

God's power follows the Word, and it makes the devil mad. Sometimes the devil will manifest himself through someone in the service, and if you are the speaker, that is where your authority and power comes in. Do not let the devil have any room to operate.

A few years ago, I was at a FGBMFI chapter meeting, also in Indiana. The first woman at the altar held her head at an odd angle. As soon as I cast the devil out of her body, her head straightened right up, and she began praising Jesus.

But a demon in the woman next to her manifested and began to say, "I won't come out of her. You can't make me come out of her."

After the devil says the same thing three or four times, it begins to "bug" you. I excused myself from the congregation, gathered a few people around the woman who knew how to exercise faith, and began to command the demon to come out of her.

All of a sudden, she began to cry, and a denominational pastor who was there jumped up, took his wife by the hand, and said, "Let's get out of here."

Do Not Apologize for the Word

I did not stop him. I do not apologize for God, and I do not explain what He is doing — unless the Lord tells me to do so. Regardless of what we believe, God is still on the throne, and the Bible is still true. If we do not get anything out of the Word, it is because we did not approach it correctly. Do not apologize for doing what the Word tells you to do.

Get your teeth into Matthew, Mark, Luke, and John. Hang onto the Gospel, and tell Satan you've got it. I guarantee God will begin to teach you. But you have to watch your religious relatives, or they will talk you out of your healing or your deliverance.

Of course, you do not want to offend them, but you are not obligated to answer their questions. Just think the way the Holy Spirit thinks.

That pastor just left. If he had simply gotten up and left because he had no understanding of what was going on or out of fear because casting out demons was unfamiliar to him, then he probably would have been all right. But the next morning, he began to judge what went on and to make fun of it from his pulpit in front of seven hundred people.

He said, "I saw something last night that was insulting to my intelligence. I do not want any of you to ever go hear a man named Norvel Hayes. He thinks he can make the devil obey. Also, I do not want any of you to ever attend a FGBMFI meeting. I only went because I heard Mr. Hayes was of our denomination, and the meeting was good until the end, until he acted like he could tell the devil what to do."

About a year later, there was a monthly meeting of the FGBMFI in that same place, and a man in dirty, ragged clothes came walking up to the front at the invitation.

He said, "I was here a year ago, and you had a speaker named Norvel Hayes. He cast a devil out of a woman. I didn't understand what he was doing, and I made fun of him and warned my people not to go near him again. From that day on, my life began to go down. I began to lose everything.

"I lost my church, my wife and child, and I started drinking. Here I am tonight, fallen from a salvation-preaching pastor to a wretched half-drunken guy who roams the streets alone. Please pray for me. I repent before God. I am dying. I need to be restored, and I know this is where my downfall started — making fun of the Gospel."

I am relating this story because I would like all who read this book to remember that they are responsible to the Gospel and to the Lord and not to men.

If you *know* that you have power and authority, you can make a demon leave, especially if the oppressed person has come to a gospel service and come to the altar. The person has to want to be free. Until the person gets sick and tired of that demon, there is no use for you to try to make the devil leave him.

No doubt that preacher was a good man, but he saw something new, something no one had ever taught him from the Word. But he should have been taught. It is in the Word.

In Mark 1:23-25, you see it happening in Jesus' day. He was in "church" (synagogue), and a demon in someone began screaming out. It happened then, and it happens now.

Again, I want to say that no matter how long you have been involved in deliverance, sometimes you will run into things that you do not know how to handle. However, you can always begin to pray in the Spirit, and receive answers. If you want to stay built up in God, edify yourself by praying in tongues.

You can deal with demon powers by praying in tongues. If one of your children is demon oppressed, you can make demons leave by praying in tongues, even if the child is not present. If a friend is not present but is oppressed, you can at least bind that demon and pray for them. You can turn from an ordinary Christian into a spiritual giant just through prayer and worship.

The Spirit Knows How To Get Victory

The devil cannot stand against God's power. And remember: Where the devil has been before and done damage, he will try to come back. If you are cured of alcoholism, but you used to love whiskey, the same demon will return again and again and try to tempt you to just take one drink. He will tempt you with the sin that he knows is your weakness.

I admire anyone delivered from the world of society. I know what social drinking is like. It is not easy to get delivered from all of that. I made up my mind I would not go back into that kind of life after I got saved, and it cost me my family.

Some people will not give up the world of cocktails and social life because they want to be with the "big shots." Porterhouse steaks, cocktails, and dirty jokes — that's what I was delivered from (not the steaks, but the rest of it).

Praying in tongues will keep you strong enough in God that the devil cannot drag you back.

I was in the ministry of helps for many years before God called me to public speaking. He sent me down to the town dump to pass out tracts. When He called me to public speaking, He told me He would be with me day and night, and He has been.

The things you cannot figure out, call out to God and pray in tongues. The Spirit of God knows how to get victory in every instance. If you will let Him come through you and pray in tongues, He knows how to get the will of God in every situation.

You can be sick in any form or fashion, and the prayer of faith in Jesus' name will get you your healing.

A sixteen-year-old girl called a prayer-counseling line once and asked for help. She said something was making her try to kill her relatives. Her father belonged to a motorcycle gang, and her mother was a prostitute. So the prayer-line leaders called the girl's home and found that, yes, she had tried to kill her aunt with a knife. Apparently, she was totally demon possessed.

The people manning the telephone service did not know how to handle this, so they called me. I went to see this girl and got her to come to church. She looked like a "Miss Teenage America." The girl was beautiful just like her mother, who looked like a movie star.

When the girl and I were introduced before church, I said, "Nice to know you," and she replied, "I'll kill you!"

I said, "No, you won't. I don't die easy." Then I asked her, "Do you want me to pray for you?"

She said there was nothing wrong with her and that she did *not* want me to pray for her. Many people would have left when she said she did not want prayer. But I learned a long time ago that you have to trick the devil sometimes. So I acted as if I were not going to pray for her.

So we took her into a Sunday school room where we sat around and talked. Then, all of a sudden, I grabbed her head and said, "Satan, in Jesus' name, you let her loose."

When I did, she jumped into the air and said, "Ouch! Don't do that!"

At that, I went into the hall and told the people who had brought her that it was going to take some time to get that thing out of her.

"Are you willing to stay until I get her free?" I asked, and they said they would stay as long as it took.

About that time, the girl came out where we were and said that when I prayed for her a big, black thing jumped out of her and stood in front of her.

She said, "I went weak, but when Norvel let me go, it jumped back on me again. What is that thing?"

I heard the music begin for the church service, so I suggested we go on up for the service. This was a good church, but they did not cast out demons. We were sitting on the front row on the aisle.

The pastor began to read the Bible, and the girl said to me, "Tell him I said to be quiet."

That shocked me, and I said, "Who?"

She said, "Him, the pastor. I don't want to hear him."

I told her, "You be quiet yourself!"

But a few seconds later, she said it again, "Please make him stop. It's not true. It's not true. Please tell him to stop. I don't want to hear it. I want to scream."

Finally, the pastor finished his Bible reading, and she said, "Oh, good!"

A young evangelist from Florida was the revival speaker. He was bold, and when he began to read the Bible, the girl got upset again. She wanted me to tell him to be quiet, but I kept telling her to shut up and sit still.

Then she decided she wanted a drink of water. Devils always want water. So we went for a drink of water. She tried to get away, but I dragged her back to the Sunday school room.

Her relatives had said that if she got away, she would run up on the mountain in the woods and dance all night long. They said demons would come get her every night at midnight and make her dance. At sun-up, she would lose her strength and the demonic energy would lift. She would come walking back home and sleep all day long. She had not slept in her own bed one night in three months.

When I closed the door, she looked at a picture on the wall and said, "I bet you think the devil's in me, don't you?"

I said, "What do you think I think?"

Then her voice broke. You can be possessed, but there is a part of you — the spirit man, the real you — that the devil can never take over. That part of you always yearns to be free. But when a demon is allowed into your body, it will run you.

She said, "I know it's the devil that is in me. I wish he would leave me alone. I'm just a slave!"

Then I knew that she really wanted to be free, but she did not know how. Then I knew I could get it out of her, and the Lord taught me something new that night. The demon in that girl could not stand the Bible, but I had never had any experience before that would have shown me that.

So I asked her again if she wanted me to pray, and the demon took over again and said, "No! I keep telling you I don't want you to pray."

Again, I tricked that demon. I casually walked over close to her, then grabbed her by the head.

I pulled her face up to me and said, "In Jesus' name, you get out of her, you demon."

When I turned her loose, she screamed and ran into a corner of the room. About that time, the young evangelist walked in with his Bible in his hand. I realized the Holy Spirit had sent him in there, so I told him to read the Bible out loud. It did not matter what he read, all of the Word is full of power. So he began to read hard and strong for about ten minutes, and the girl was in the corner all that time.

But she experienced one of the most beautiful conversions I have ever seen. After a few minutes of hearing the Word, I saw a tear come out of her eyes. Then her body began to slide down the wall very slowly, inch by inch. The boy was still reading the Bible. Then she began to cry real hard for about fifteen minutes.

Suddenly she stopped crying, picked herself up slowly, and we saw her face for the first time. Sitting in the corner, all of her long hair had hidden her face. Now she looked like a different person. She looked like an angel.

She said, "I'm free! They're all gone. I'm not a slave anymore. I'm free."

She reached up, hugged my neck, and laid her head on my shoulder, and right there, the Lord filled her with the Holy Spirit.

That night I learned that the Bible is more powerful than Satan and all of his demons. The devil cannot stand against the Word of God. The Word will put the devil on the run. The Word will bring the presence of the Holy Spirit onto a person, and when His presence goes on a person, the devil has to leave.

The Word of God is powerful enough to set free the demon possessed. The Word of God is powerful enough to heal the sick. His Word will never fail. His Word is not weak;

it is strong and powerful. The Word of God will set people free.

8

Demons Do Not Obey Weak Christians

Devils do not listen to weak Christians. He beats them to the ground in spite of the authority Jesus has given them. Having authority and exercising it are two different things.

Once I was in Fort Wayne, Indiana, again speaking to a FGBMFI convention. After I spoke, the Holy Spirit caught me up in heavenly glory. My prayer turned into prophecy and went on about twelve minutes.

I was just speaking words as the Spirit gave them to me. Then someone began crying and crying, but I kept my eyes closed. When I finished, I opened my eyes, and about forty people were in front of me being healed.

Do not be worried about the appearance of people who come to church. God will deal with that. It is not your business. Do not worry about the outward person. Be concerned about the inward man.

I have seen some people so messed up that even the devil did not want them. When you get too bad, the devil's crowd does not want you anymore.

Just remember that Jesus will accept you the way you are, if you will bow down before Him and ask for mercy. Ask for mercy, and you will get it. If you do not want to get involved in casting out devils because it is "weird," you are already involved in weird stuff — and that weird stuff is you.

Casting out demons and laying hands on the sick is supposed to be the normal Christian life. Learn about the power that is in you. The Holy Spirit does not think as we think. He thinks according to the reality of heaven: no sickness, no confusion, no nervousness, no cripples, and no blindness.

Until you get your mind renewed with the Word of God and stop thinking about yourself, you cannot even get healed.

Remember: the Holy Spirit is not ignorant. If you are not receiving the blessings of God, it should be evident to you that you *are* ignorant. The Kingdom of God is total victory, and if you are born again, you have inherited heaven. The entire Kingdom of Heaven lives in you.

God Blesses Yielded People

God only blesses people mightily who want to learn and who will yield themselves to God. It is hard to get free from the devil if you go to a church where they refuse to cast out demons.

Luke 9:1 says that Jesus has given His disciples all power and authority over all devils and over all sicknesses and diseases. *All* devils include the ones that have been robbing you of heaven's blessings. (Also see Matt. 28:18-20.) You have a right to be free.

Do I think the Lord will heal you? *Yes,* I know that He already has healed you. Healing, as well as salvation and freedom from demonic influences, was provided on the cross. However, just as you have to choose salvation and believe on Jesus to receive, you must receive healing. If you will not believe the Scriptures, you will not be able to receive healing.

Faith is not believing what can be seen, but believing what is not seen *because the Word says it.* If you want to be free of demonic oppression, act and talk like you are free.

God will honor what you do in His Son's name, but not a false doctrine.

Wondering in your mind and wavering to and fro between opinions (are there demons, and can I be free of this oppression?) will put you in an early grave. If you are a pastor afraid to cast out demons because you might lose some members, obey the Word of God and let those go who want to go. The Lord will bless you for obedience.

The Lord told me one day, "Son, do you want to know what real faith is? You have been teaching it, you ought to learn what it is. Anything you will give Me thanks for with joy and not let your mind wonder, I will see to it that you get it."

Always remember, He loves you as much as He loves me. You need something, you start thanking Him for it right now and every day. One day, all of a sudden, you will have it. Let Jesus hear you thanking Him.

I bought a block of property in Cleveland, Tennessee, for the Bible school. I paid $10,000 down on it, and for a year and a half, money came floating in from everywhere. I never took up an offering. I have bought property the Lord told me to and built buildings the Lord told me to, and never took up an offering.

Money to pay for those things just came in. People would call and say the Lord had told them to give me certain amounts of money. I raised money for our children's home. For God to perform financial miracles, He has to have time. He does not mint money in heaven and drop it down to you. He has to work through the world's systems, so it takes time to work out circumstances.

However, if you keep giving Him thanks for anything He promised you in the New Testament, continually, every day — and do it joyfully and reverently, in Jesus' name — He will get that thing for you. You must be bold and loud. That is the only way I know to do it.

Be Bold and Loud

When I have a need in my life and go to God in Jesus' name, thanking Him, He gives it to me. He hears me, the devil hears me, and the neighbors hear me! I am telling you, this works.

Jesus said to me once, "Son, if you will get people who are devil possessed to confess their freedom, they will get free quicker. If you say, 'In Jesus' name, come out of him,' and nothing happens, get them to thank God for their freedom."

If you believe Jesus and thank Him for what He has promised, He will do anything for you. But do not forget to thank Him for everything he has promised — that means, in advance. Faith means "in advance" believe you have something. Begin to thank God for it before you ever see it.

Do not ask God how He is going to do it, or decide He is going to do this or that. That is departing from faith. When you try to figure God out, you are departing from faith. Boldly and totally throw yourself over on Jesus, claim what you need or want, and God's power will come on you and give you what you want. But you must do it every day.

Faith in God's desire to bless you and His ability and willingness to do so is a way of life, not a one-time occurrence.

Unless you resist and rebuke the devil, demons are not going to go anywhere, ever. Do not be ashamed of the Gospel or the power of Jesus' name. It does not matter how you feel or do not feel. Every day, resist the devil in Jesus' name.

You cannot cast out demons without faith.

You cannot cast out demons without the Word.

You cannot cast out demons without boldness.

The Holy Spirit inside you knows all truth, has all knowledge of heaven, and has all the power you need to operate in the authority you have been given.

Those who seek Him will find Him.

It is an awful thing for a ten-year-old to have his mother die, then stand by the coffin and try not to cry. I loved her so much, and I did not want to say goodbye. My mother died of cancer at the age of thirty-seven. That is why I am so bold and ruthless against the devil, and particularly against cancer.

You have to *make* it get out of you. Cancer is a work of hell. All diseases come from the devil. All heartaches come from the devil. All spirits that entice your children into taking drugs or becoming alcoholics come from the devil.

But Jesus came down from heaven to bring us eternal life and life more abundantly here on earth. Stick with Jesus, and you will have a life full of peace, joy, and power over the enemy. Whom the Son sets free is free indeed. (John 8:36.) God wants you free to believe the whole Bible, not just the parts that fit the doctrines of men.

Some denominations have not departed from the doctrine of salvation, yet they are not believing the *whole* Bible because they have departed from the doctrine of healing and the doctrine of deliverance.

Whatever Jesus did is what I want to do. Jesus is the Head of the Church. All pastors are "undershepherds" of the Lord Jesus Christ. All pastors are supposed to obey Jesus and do what He did. Then, as a member of a local church, you are to obey your pastor in Christ. However, you do have a right to check on what your pastor is preaching to see if he is obeying Jesus or not.

A good pastor will want you to bring your Bible to church and check up on him. Once I went to a minister's conference where I was a speaker. I wanted to have a healing service. But the Lord said He wanted me to have a deliverance service.

So I had to go in there in front of full-gospel ministers, speak on deliverance, and then minister deliverance. I spoke and gave an invitation. Some one hundred and fifty people jumped out of their seats and came down front. And I taught the pastor and the evangelist holding this conference.

I said, "See all these people? Outwardly, they look as if they are in pretty good shape. But I have not prayed yet. It is amazing how good a church looks until you have a deliverance service."

So I began to pray and bind the devil in Jesus' name. And demons began to scream out in those people. They began to fight and to fall on the floor. A demon can be in you for twenty years and never scream and fight as long as you do what he wants. He will not manifest twenty-four hours a day — only whenever he needs to in order to keep you in line.

9
The Sign of Holiness

The sign of holiness is not any outward appearance, but is keeping your mouth shut and obeying Matthew, Mark, Luke, and John; loving everybody; praying, and reading your Bible. The sign of holiness is walking in faith in everything you do.

Faith means obedience. When you obey God, you have faith. When Jesus tells you to do something, and you do it, that shows God you have faith in His Son. If you do not show Him by your works that you have faith, you are going to have nothing but trouble. Then you will be wondering why good things do not come your way.

Show God that you can be contented where you are and patient. If you are contented and patient, that is a sign you know God. I am never sure that nervous people know God. God is not nervous.

Obedience means faithfulness in doing what the Word says, answering whatever call is on your life, and being a good steward of your time, as well as your money. If you are not a good steward of God's money, your bills will never be paid. Do not spend your life wondering what God is going to do. If you can read, then you should know what He is going to do. He is going to confirm Matthew, Mark, Luke, and John. God is not going to write any new books to the Bible for you.

For two thousand years, He has been confirming Matthew, Mark, Luke, and John for those who believe it. You can have your own doctrine if you want to, but nothing but God's is successful.

If you are not successful, do not check up on God. There is nothing wrong with Him. Check up on yourself. The Bible is never wrong. Jesus is never wrong. Health-wise, lost children-wise, finance-wise, mind-wise. Check up on why you are not enjoying the blessings of God.

You want to cast out devils? Build yourself up and use your heavenly language. He gives it to you for several reasons: the first, to talk to Him with; and the second, to edify yourself, to build up yourself. If you do that, you will be doing what God says to do.

If you are sick, Jesus will heal you — every time for everybody — if they will receive it. But you have no right to judge God by how He deals with your friends. Once you refuse to do what Jesus tells you, refuse to trust Him and do your own thing, that is when you allow seducing devils and doctrines of devils to come in and cause you to believe all sorts of things.

Faith is not seen. I do not cast out demons because I see or smell or feel something. I cast them out because the Word of God tells me to cast them out. It is by faith that you do things for God. When you depart from faith, you open the door for seducing spirits. Your mind is in danger of being sucked up by the devil. Because you are not believing the right thing, you will accept the wrong thing.

God does not honor wondering. He honors faith. If Jesus tells you to do something, you had better do it. Right before Jesus went to heaven, He said, . . . **they shall lay hands on the sick, and they shall recover . . .** (Mark 16:18). Then He went right on to heaven.

Yet there are ministers who will tell their congregations, "That's not the way we do things around here."

I know God does not think too highly of that attitude. If you refuse to obey Jesus, you are in trouble with God already. It does not matter what is involved. Get started in obedience. Nothing is too difficult or too hard for the Lord.

No Cases Are Too Hard for God

In the late Seventies, I was preaching at a big church in Dallas, Texas, when this girl came running down the aisle, screaming. After we got her delivered, she told us that she had hitchhiked there because she had heard I was to speak. She had heard that I made devils leave people, and she was a lesbian.

Demons that infest lesbians and homosexuals or drug addicts do not always give up easily. To stay clean, the people must receive the right kind of teaching. The love of God saturated that girl, and the demons left. But they kept trying to come back for a long time.

She showed up in Cleveland, Tennessee, at the Bible school I started. For a while she would be okay, then she would go back into that oppression. She went back and forth for months. We kept loving and talking to her. We would talk and lay hands on her and pray. Then those spirits would try to get her again.

Once, she stood in the parking lot during services for days. She would not come inside. This went on for more than a year. We could not keep her still long enough to get the teaching in her. But we just kept on and on, in patience. Today, she is full of the love of the Lord.

At the graduation banquet the next year, I said, "I'm proud of all of you students, but I think I am most proud of little Trudy. The greatest thing in the world is the love of God. It is amazing what you can do with love."

No matter what the devil tries, if there is someone who loves you and keeps persisting, the devil will lose. Sometimes the flesh gets tired, but the Holy Spirit never gets tired of loving.

It is wonderful to see what God does. The greatest thrill of my life was seeing my daughter sitting on the front row at church and Christian meetings, and later, seeing her get up and speak at meetings. For three years, I went through hell with her. She did not darken the door of the church during that time. She would not even go to one service.

Sometimes a case may seem hopeless. But the love of Jesus works for everybody. Just keep loving them, but do not allow those people to cause confusion for others.

Fred Price, pastor of Crenshaw Christian Center in California, is strict with those who take leadership positions in his church. He has more than ten thousand members, and he has strict rules like you would not believe.

A girl came to him who had an advanced degree in music and wanted to participate in the music program at his church.

He said, "That's fine. You sit on the front pew for two years, and maybe after a year, I might let you sing in the choir. Then, if you are faithful in the choir, I might let you sing a solo."

If you are asked to participate in church, you ought to be so thrilled. It is an honor for you and me to have the privilege of doing something for God. If you want to sing, you had better be just as satisfied singing in the nursing home as on Sunday morning in front of the church.

Many times, old people in those homes are oppressed by demons. One song or one prayer can set them free. Do not think yourself too good to make visits to nursing homes and jails. If you cannot preach, you can at least give your own testimony in detail.

Two Ways To Cast Out Devils

There are two ways to cast out devils: one is to say "come out of him"; the other is to say "go"!

But both ways require faith and obedience, the signs of holiness. You cannot do anything without faith. You must have faith in the name of Jesus and faith that the name is more powerful than all devils. Your faith in Jesus' name can get victory for the person you are praying for.

Every bad thing that happens is the work of hell, but the work of hell has to bow to the authority of the name of Jesus. On earth, the closest thing to hell you will ever see is your state mental institution.

Take a stroll through one some time. See the shape the patients are in. Some will laugh, some will hide, some will be bold. All are full of devils making fun of God. Many of the people do not know where they are, so much of them has been taken over by the devil.

As I said earlier, however, their demonic oppression usually began with some misuse of the body. What you do with your body affects your mind. For years and years, all of the mental patients with whom I have worked have done strange things with or to their bodies.

A person involved in addictions, perversions, or compulsions will eventually lose his mind. He will lose all self-respect. His thoughts will get fuzzy. One of these days, his mind will snap. Regular hospitals may have empty beds, but most mental institutions in America have long waiting lists.

If you will give your life to the Lord Jesus Christ, keep your body full of the Holy Spirit, and praise the name of Jesus, your mind will never snap. But even lying, cheating, and gossiping will affect your mind eventually. You will not be able to know the truth when you hear it because you have given place to a lying, deceiving spirit.

Your body is the temple of the Holy Spirit. God wants you to have a sound mind, a mind full of peace, power, love, and joy. Begin doing strange things with your body, and you will totally lose the precious life of the Spirit.

Teach your children how important it is to have friends who are godly. Turn your children away from the wrong crowd.

We were passing out tracts once, and a girl said, "Stay away from me!"

We said, "We just want to give you a tract and tell you Jesus loves you."

She said, "I know all about God. I used to sing in the choir and attend a church. Every Sunday, when the doors were open, I was there. I was a 'goody, goody' all my life. And I got tired of it. I wanted to see what the rest of the world offered. But I didn't want to become like this."

We said, "Jesus loves you. You can repent."

She replied, "No, He doesn't love me! Jesus doesn't love me. I've gone too far. I've committed the unpardonable sin. I live in the valley of the damned forever."

"In Jesus' name," we said, "you *can* be free."

She said, "No, I can't be free. But, mister, please tell all the young people you see everywhere not to get tired of going to church and singing in the choir. Don't get tired of going to church and being good.

"You see that girl on the corner over there walking back and forth like a mad dog? I'm 'married' to that girl. And she's mad because I'm talking to you. So you see, I'm damned," she said, and whirled around, disappearing into the dark. She was doomed.

All she would have had to do was fall on her knees and ask Jesus to forgive her and make her clean. So many people believe what the devil says and think they are too bad to come back. But I'm telling you the Spirit of God can break the shackles of sin.

You can be a totally free human being who can praise Jesus from your innermost being. Do not ever leave the doctrine of faith because if you do, you will get messed up for sure. Showing your faith in Jesus is what brings you victory every time.

Keep yourself filled with the Holy Spirit so that you have the power to cast out devils.

> For he that speaketh in an unknown tongue speaketh not unto men, but unto God: for no man understandeth him; howbeit in the spirit he speaketh mysteries.
>
> 1 Corinthians 14:2

First of all, God gave you your heavenly language to talk to Him with. If you speak in an unknown tongue, you edify yourself. You build yourself in God. You become strong. The devils are weak. If you build yourself up, you will be able to exercise in power the authority Jesus left us.

Do not attend a church that makes fun of tongues and of casting out devils. That church is making fun of the Gospel. Go where the Lord has freedom.

A young lady from Nashville, Tennessee, was being interviewed on the *700 Club* once by Ben Kinchlow.

She said, "My sister who lives in another state called me not long ago and said she was coming to visit me and bringing me a big gift. I was in fear of everything, and I thought perhaps she was bringing me a German Shepherd to help guard my house.

"But when my sister arrived, she said the 'gift' was a guy who lived about three hours away, and his name was Norvel Hayes. She said he has a school and sanctuary in Cleveland, and her gift was a trip to see him. She said the Lord told her I was supposed to go there.

"It had been odd enough to hear her say she was praying for me. But taking me to see a man who casts out devils was even odder," the girl said.

They made an appointment with me, but when the girl and her sister arrived, it was time for a service. I was busy, so they went into the church for the meeting.

The girl said, "As soon as Mr. Hayes began to speak, he began to speak on the devil and demons. I knew very quickly that was what was wrong with me."

Until then, she had never identified her problems with the devil. However, he is behind all phobias and all diseases. And a Christian has power to resist devils and make them leave, in Jesus' name.

She told Ben Kinchlow, "As Mr. Hayes spoke, everything got real quiet. Then he gave an invitation, and my sister went up front. I wondered what she was going up for, but she was told there was someone in her family who needed to be healed. I was still sitting in my seat, and all of a sudden, something warm came into my body.

"Then it turned from warm to hot. All of a sudden, that hot spot blew up. When it did, everything left me, and my body was filled with joy. All demons left me. All fear left me. Everything oppressive left me, and it has been that way ever since."

The Spirit of God does what you believe and what you teach that is aligned with the Word.

You must keep yourself built up and not let the devil run rampant in your life. Bind him up and throw him out. Do not accept anything except victory. Do not allow yourself to be satisfied with anything except total victory.

Norvel Hayes shares God's Word boldly and simply, with an enthusiasm that captures the heart of the hearer. He has learned through personal experience that God's Word can be effective in every area of life and that it will work for anyone who will believe it and apply it.

Norvel owns several businesses which function successfully despite the fact that he spends more than half his time away from the office, ministering the Gospel throughout the country. His obedience to God and his willingness to share his faith have taken him to a variety of places. He ministers in churches, seminars, conventions, colleges, prisons — anywhere the Spirit of God leads.

To contact Norvel Hayes, write:

Norvel Hayes
P. O. Box 1379
Cleveland, TN 37311

Please include your prayer requests when you write.

Books by Norvel Hayes

How To Live and Not Die

*The Winds of God
Bring Revival*

*God's Power Through
the Laying on of Hands*

The Blessing of Obedience

*Stand in the Gap
for Your Children*

*How To Get
Your Prayers Answered*

Holy Spirit Gifts Series

*Number One Way
To Fight the Devil*

*Why You Should
Speak in Tongues*

Prostitute Faith

*You Must Confess
Your Faith*

What To Do for Healing

*God's Medicine of Faith —
The Word*

*How To Triumph
Over Sickness*

*Financial Dominion —
How To Take Charge
of Your Finances*

The Healing Handbook

*Rescuing Souls
From Hell —
Handbook for
Effective Soulwinning*

How To Cast Out Devils

Power for Living

Radical Christianity

*Secrets to Keeping
Your Faith Strong*

*Putting Your Angels
To Work*

Additional copies of *Know Your Enemy,*
or any other books by Norvel Hayes,
are available from your local bookstore,
or by writing:

Harrison House
P. O. Box 35035
Tulsa, OK 74153